Flight Attendant Interview Questions
By Sara Keagle

www.theflightattendantcourse.com

"You only have one chance to make a first impression. Remember that the recruiters may be all around the building you are interviewing in. You have no idea who you'll be speaking with, so assume that each person you come in contact with might be making a decision. There will always be that one candidate that might not get an offer because of something that was observed outside of the actual interview process. ex) talking loudly on a cell phone, cursing when someone might hear you, inappropriate conversations not suitable for a business setting, not seeming to be interested in what others are saying, setting up a complete "beauty salon" in a public restroom, arriving in overly casual attire and changing in a public restroom, etc."

-recruiter of a major U.S. Airline

Flight attendant applicants are being continually observed from the time they enter the building, sometimes even before:

"Hey all! I'm in total shock. I was waiting for the hotel van and started chatting with a young guy who was dressed in ripped jeans and had total attitude. He was cussing and being loud and obnoxious. Turns out he just non-revved in (non-rev is flying stand by). Don't they send these recruits the dress code info anymore? Who do I talk to about him?"

This was posted in a flight attendant forum of a major airline. Whether you think the person who posted is right or wrong...as someone aspiring to become a flight attendant, it is in your best interest to be fully aware that people are not only watching, they're also talking! As a side note, if you strongly believe that you should be able to dress and speak as you please (this is America after all) you might want to reconsider whether or not this is the right career choice for you. As a flight attendant you are the front line employee, you are the face of the airline...uniform or not. Something to ponder and always keep in mind.

The key to the entire interview process is to be authentic. Every recruiter I interviewed had one thing in common: they are looking for flight attendant candidates that are a good fit for the airline. They can see through the practiced responses. The best thing you can do to prepare for the interview questions is to know thy self and know why you'd make a great flight attendant. The trick is to ask yourself ahead of time, to think of real life scenarios and be able to tell the story.

• What is your education?

• Give an example of when you went above and beyond for a customer.

• Give an example of a stressful situation and how you handled it.

- What positions have you held that demanded flexibility and how did you deal with that challenge?

- Give an example of a time in your life when you've had to adapt.

- What situations have you been in that would demonstrate you are service oriented?

- Describe an example of a time when you had to demonstrate teamwork.

- What will be the most challenging aspect about the flight attendant lifestyle for you?

- Describe a time that you were able to diffuse a difficult situation.

- Do you speak a second language?

Meeting the Interviewer:

It is essential that you are able to look the recruiters in the eye, speak clearly and loudly enough to be heard. This not only shows confidence, but also shows that you will be able to present yourself well to customers.

The interviewers are looking at both your appearance and how you carry yourself. They are looking for poise, confidence and a positive, friendly attitude. Approachability is key. Be mindful of your posture and smile 'til it hurts! I've actually had recruiters tell me the answers to the questions are secondary to how the candidate makes them feel.

They are looking at you through the eyes of their customers. So, ask yourself:

"How am I being seen?"

"Would I want to be greeted onto the aircraft by me?"

Role Play

A great activity to try is to ask your friends and family how you come across to them. Ask them if you are warm, friendly and approachable. More importantly ask them where you can improve. Let them know you are not searching for compliments and that constructive criticism is appreciated.

You can also practice in the mirror! The more the better! If you can get comfortable talking to yourself in the mirror, you will be comfortable talking with anyone! It will help loosen you up for the video interview especially.

Role play with a friend or family member, be both the flight attendant candidate and the recruiter. It is always a good idea to get the other sides perspective. It will help you understand what they are looking for and why. Use the questions in this workbook and conduct an interview!

You do not want to go into your interview feeling unprepared or unsure about how you present yourself.

How to answer questions about the flight attendant job

Questions pertaining specifically to the flight attendant profession can be tricky, especially if you haven't had any experience in the industry. Some airlines will send out a questionnaire after you submit your application with the type of questions listed below. The key to answering these questions is to use common sense. The questions may be in a multiple choice format and seem repetitive. This is because they want to see if you are consistent with your answers and if you have good common sense on how to deal with situations that may come your way at 35k ft! Keep in mind, it's you and your crew up there. It's up to you to figure out how to handle things that are not everyday problems. Anything and everything seems to happen up there! So, how do you prepare for every possible thing? You really can't, which is why the airline is relying on flight attendants that have common sense, are good team players and know how to think outside the box! Here are some examples of the questions you may be asked on a questionnaire or even in an actual interview. I'm giving specific answers on these questions, but I still don't recommend that you memorize them. I'm hoping that the answer makes sense to you so you are able to recognize this type of question and answer accordingly.

- **What would you do if you saw one of your coworkers treating the passengers badly?**

I would step in and tell the worker that he/she was needed in the galley and give them a minute to calm down. I would also tell them that I will finish helping the passenger with their needs and be polite to the passenger.

- **What would you do if a child refuses to get in their seat after the door is closed?**

Informing the individuals who are traveling with the child is important. Letting them know the door has closed and that the child needs to be seated for safety is important. I would also talk to the child in a playful voice and tell them that we are getting ready to go and that they need to be seated before the plane can move.

- **What would you do if the plane has been sitting on the tarmac for 2 hours and the passengers are getting restless?**

Keeping the passengers in the loop of things is important today. I would ask the captain to make an updated announcement with any new information. I would also try to help passengers by offering them lavatory usage, water, and the ability to use any cellular devices if approved by the captain.

- **What would you do if one of your coworkers is not pulling their weight on the plane?**

I would ask the employee for help and let them know that we are all tried and that a break can take place after the passenger needs.

- **What would you do if one of your coworkers was taking or stealing food from the plane after everyone else has deplaned?**

I would approach the employee and casually ask if they needed me to ring them up for their purchase before we left the aircraft so that no one gets in trouble.

- **What would you do if one of the passengers refuses to comply with the seatbelt and electronic device mandates?**

First I would remind the passenger that the seatbelt sign is on and that the electronic devices needed to be placed in airplane mode or

*turned off. If the passenger does not comply I would let the lead flight attendant know about the problem and also **inform** the captain.*
(Key to this question is to inform not enforce)

Flight Attendants play a key role in safety onboard the aircraft, but it's important to understand that they are not law enforcement, they are informers not enforcers. Should the aircraft or anyone onboard be in imminent danger, obviously a flight attendant's role would adapt and they would do what they need to do, including looking to other crew members and passengers for assistance.

At the Interview

Tell us about yourself and tell us about a time you had an unhappy customer. How did you handle that situation?

This is a common question (or a similar version) asked in group settings at a flight attendant group interview. There is a good chance you will be asked to stand up in front of the group and answer a question similar to the one above.

Think now about how you feel about standing up in front of a large group of people and answering these questions. Are you nervous? Don't worry! They are not looking for professional public speakers.

Let's break it down

Tell us a little bit about yourself:

This is your chance to shine! You don't want to ramble, so the best thing you can do is prepare. Prepare a few talking points about yourself:

• Name

• Where are you from

- What is your current job or are you a student

- Talk briefly about any jobs you've had in customer service

- Why would you make a great flight attendant

- What abilities do you possess that qualify you to be a flight attendant

- Are there any volunteer positions you've had that could be viewed as relevant experience

- Do you speak a second language

Once you've answered these questions and added in any relevant information about yourself, you'll want to get comfortable talking about yourself. You don't want this to be too practiced, it's more of a guideline for you to follow. A list, that will help you remember all of the topics you think will be relevant and applicable.

The recruiters will be interested in how authentically you answer the questions. Does your answer appear memorized or sincere? Did you understand the issue your customer was having and were you able to solve it in a mutually satisfying way?

How should this be answered? Using the **STAR** Method

STAR (Situation, Task, Action, Result)

This type of question requires more than a yes or no answer. Using the STAR method to answer it will help you give the recruiters what they are looking for: a complete answer that shows you know how to problem solve.

- *Should go without saying: never roll your eyes at any other candidates' answers. Give everyone the same consideration you would like to be given; remember you are being watched.*

- *Don't ever put down a previous employer or customer. Avoid negatives at all costs.*

The Questions

Please keep in mind that the airlines are changing up the questions all the time; these are just examples for you to go by. They have all been asked at a major U.S. airline interview at one time or another. I won't give you exact answers, but rather different ways to help you think of how you would answer the questions based on your own experiences. The last thing you want to do is memorize a bunch of answers because you think they are the "right" answers. As mentioned before, recruiters know practiced answers! Even worse would be to memorize and count on questions that never get asked. Going over these examples will help you prepare for any questions the recruiter may throw out to you.

"Are you willing to relocate?"

There is only one correct answer to this question. Give a sincere **YES** and elaborate only if you are excited about the opportunity to go anywhere and everywhere; otherwise move on. This is not the right time to ask questions about relocating. I can't stress this enough. Many recruiters have passed over otherwise perfect applicants because they sensed their reluctance to move.

"Why do you want to be a flight attendant for 'Xyz' airline?"

By now you've done your research. You have educated yourself on the positive aspects of the airlines to which you are applying and should be able to answer this one on your own. It's a personal question that truly, only you can answer.

"What do you think the primary responsibility of a flight attendant is? "

Safety is the primary responsibility of flight attendants, followed by meeting the needs of the customers and ensuring their comfort on board the aircraft.

"What makes a good flight attendant? "

Excellent customer service, outgoing, dependable, good listener, team player, flexible...all of these work. Add more by thinking of what qualities **you** have that would make **you** a great flight attendant.

"How would you deal with an angry customer? "

First and foremost you want to acknowledge their frustration and make sure they feel heard. Think back to a time that you helped an angry customer; this would be a good time to use that story as an example of how you would handle a situation like this.

"What does customer service mean to you?"

Again go on your personal experiences. When did you provide great customer experience and how did it make you feel? Use this example and talk about the pride you felt. Choose service oriented words like, "anticipating the customers' needs", "being service oriented", you like to "go the extra mile", you "enjoy making people feel special" etc...

"If a customer complained about the airline, how would you handle it? "

You want to show here that you can turn a negative into a positive. Are you proactive? Give an example of how you turned a situation around. Remember, they are looking for problem solvers, they want to know that you have the skills necessary to work unsupervised and deal with any issues you encounter onboard the aircraft.

"What special skills do you have that would benefit you as a flight attendant? "

This would be a time to highlight any safety skills you possess. Were you ever a life guard? Do you know CPR? Are you culturally aware? Do you speak a second language...including sign language? Anything that gives you an extra edge and is a skill you can see yourself using onboard is worth mentioning.

"Why do you want to be a flight attendant?"

Why do you? Are you passionate about customer service? Are you excited about the world opening up to you? Being exposed to different people and cultures? Do you love to help people? Are you excited to be in an environment that is always changing? You can throw your love of travel in here, but make it a small part of your answer, not your whole answer. Remember, be sincere; you want your passion and excitement to show in this answer.

"You realize you won't be able to make it to work on time due to an unexpected issue, i.e. your car broke down or there is a family emergency of some kind, what do you do? "

They understand emergencies happen sometimes, they want to know you are able to handle the situation by informing crew scheduling ASAP. It is essential the airline runs on schedule, and crew scheduling needs as much time as possible to find your replacement.

"Why should we hire you?"

This is your time to brag about yourself. Go back to the questions I asked you to ask yourself. Use words that describe the skill set of a flight attendant: dependable, reliable, friendly, problem solver, team player, punctual etc....mention how excited you are for this new adventure. Be sincere and authentic and excited!

"What would you do if a passenger didn't want to sit next to another passenger due to their ethnicity or race? "

Think about how you would handle something like this. What if it was a cultural thing? What if a man doesn't want to sit next to a female that is not in his family due to his religion? What about someone not wanting to sit next to someone due to their weight? Maybe they're losing some of their seat space and are feeling quite uncomfortable. The first thing to do is not make it a personal agenda, this needs to be handled professionally. Explain that you would handle it in the most ethical way possible to avoid anyone being offended or hurt and make any and all apologies necessary. Situations like this require discretion and sometimes the input of fellow flight attendants may be helpful. If you're still at the gate, a possible remedy could be simply requesting the help of a gate agent or supervisor.

"Have you ever bent company rules at a previous job?"

If you haven't, it's perfectly ok to be honest and explain that you haven't. What might be an acceptable reason for breaking the rules? Maybe you did so to help out a customer? Again, use common sense and remember, safety is the number one priority of an airline.

"What tasks do you find to be repetitive and boring at your current job?"

Maybe you don't come in contact with customers enough? Think of things you currently do that would not be something you would handle as a flight attendant. Still explain how you may find it a little repetitive and boring, but you know they're necessary for the operation and you make the most of it by adding _____. Maybe you are able to listen to music or you can make a competition with yourself to get the job done, doing your best?

"How would you handle a customer with an unreasonable request?"

You want to convey that you would accommodate the customer in the best way possible without over stepping any boundaries or promising things you can't deliver, keeping the airline and FAA rules in the forefront.

"What are your strengths?"

Think about your strengths and back them up using adjectives that best describe what makes a great flight attendant. Use specific examples, tell a story that shows your strengths.

These are a few good examples of adjectives that you may want to use:

- motivated
- positive
- responsible
- approachable
- composed
- calm
- focused
- hard working
- patient

"What are your weaknesses?"

This is a classic question that is seemingly asking for a negative answer. Truthfully, it is designed to determine a candidates' overall outlook. Can they turn this into a positive? What ARE your weaknesses? Are you a perfectionist? Do you find it difficult to say no? Whatever your weakness is, turn it into a positive and make it clear you are aware of it and what you're doing about it. Maybe because you're a perfectionist, it takes you a long time to complete tasks. What are you doing to fix this? Maybe you could delegate more often? Maybe you allow your team more responsibility.

"What are your expectations when it comes to working for 'Xyz' Airlines?"

What are they? This is a personal question, give it some thought and be sincere in your answer. Be sure to include why it will be mutually beneficial.

"How long do you see yourself working as a flight attendant if you are successful today?"

Keep in mind the airlines are looking to invest in people that plan on sticking around for a long time. This is not the time to say, you are just planning on having fun traveling for a few years before you get your "real" life going. Believe it or not, the recruiters reported hearing that...often!

"What don't you like about your current job?"

You may be asked questions that seem negative. Don't be fooled, this is not the time to let it all out and complain about everything you hate about your job. Start with a positive, "I've enjoyed working at 'Abc company', but I feel I've grown as much as I can there." Avoid using phrases like, "I hated that they...." or "I have to get out of there because...." Stay as positive as you can and continually reiterate your reasons for wanting to be a flight attendant.

"How would you handle a situation where you can't understand a customer? "

The recruiters are looking for common sense here. Is the customer a foreigner? Perhaps there is another crew member that can help out.

Maybe you just need to repeat yourself and speak slower or more clearly. There are many ways to answer this, make it clear that you would make every effort to communicate clearly with the customer and get help if needed by offering clear examples as previously stated.

"Can you remember one example from one other candidate's response in the group setting? "

This is where you show that you have been paying attention, that you're a good listener and that you are aware of what's happening around you.

"How would you describe yourself?"

This question may also be worded as, "how would a friend describe you?". Tap into the key words listed previously that apply to you. Which of these words describes you and your character?

- flexible
- dependable
- adaptable
- team player
- organized
- detail oriented
- friendly
- optimistic
- problem solver
- safety minded

"Name a strength you bring to this airline?"

What are your strengths? Think about it now, write down all the adjectives you can think of relating to strengths that describe you and go with your strongest attribute. Have an example ready as to why you feel this way about yourself. What are you going to bring to the table?

"What kind of jobs have you had and what did you enjoy about them?"

This is a great time to show how much you love people without saying those exact words (I think it's safe to say that if you don't love people, this career is going to be tough for you!). Talk about customer service positions and give actual examples of how much you enjoyed working with customers and helping people.

"Do you know my name and title?"

Remember to listen. Easy.

"If a passenger came onboard visibly distraught, how would you handle it?"

Communication skills are key. The safety of your flight is the most important thing. You'd want to have a private conversation with the passenger and ask if there is anything you can do to help them, finding out as much as you can about the situation. If you have any doubt in your mind about their ability to get through the flight, consult your crew members for input. If the passenger seems ok, let them know you are available throughout the flight and that you will check on them periodically. Always keep the captain in the loop.

STAR Questions

Use the STAR (Situation, Task, Action, Result) method we discussed earlier to answer the following types of questions.

"Tell us about a time you have been under stress. Did you recognize it? How do you cope with stress? "

They will want to hear a specific situation in which you had to handle stress and then HOW you handled it. Explain the details of your actions during that event, then how you were able to cope and find support after the crisis has passed? Do you confront problems head on? As a flight attendant you will find yourself in situations on the aircraft (medical emergencies, passenger altercations, aircraft malfunctions etc..) that need to be handled and your stress will need to be shelved until the incident has passed or maybe not even until you are home from a trip.

Elaborate by adding the tools you have in place for dealing with stress, i.e., do you have a good support system? Friends, family or a community you can count on? Do you meditate? Exercise?

"Tell us about a time you were part of a team and worked well together."

Think back to anytime you were part of a team in a work situation where you worked together to solve an issue. Preferably customer service related. If you took charge or played a leadership role in that team setting, elaborate on that.

"Tell us about a time you had to plan for poor weather? "

They ask this question to find out if you are someone that thinks ahead. Have you been in a situation and were you prepared for it? Are you prepared for any situation? Maybe you have an emergency kit you put together and keep in your car, apartment or garage. Do you have a list of family members or friends that can help out at a moments notice?

"Tell us about a time you went above and beyond?"

Think of a situation where you went out of your way to help a customer. What was expected of you and what did you do that would be considered "above and beyond"? Be sure to clarify how you went the extra mile vs. normal expectations.

"Tell us about a time you experienced great customer service?"

This is a great question. Think back on a time that's memorable to you where you were made to feel special because of how someone went above and beyond for YOU. Tell them what happened and how it changed your state of mind. This will convey that you understand what exceptional customer service is.

"Can you tell us about a time that you had to make a quick decision? "

Think of a situation, preferably a work situation and tell the story.

"Give an example of when you had to deal with someone who comes from a different ethnic background. "

They want to know that you will show the same respect and service to all people regardless of their ethnicity. If this is a global airline you will be flying customers from all over the world. Some countries have very different views than ours in the U.S. Some you may not agree with on a personal level, but your short flight with them is not the time to try to change that or impose your belief system. Make it clear that you respect all people, all cultures and will treat everyone with dignity and respect. You can also let them know that you are motivated to learn about new cultures.

"Tell us about a time that you were not supported by your employer?"

Think of a time you felt this way. Tell them what the situation was and how you handled it. They want to know that ultimately, you did not go against your employer and that you followed all company policies and guidelines.

"Tell us about a time you dealt with a disgruntled customer."

This is a great time to show that you know how to defuse a situation. Listening is a great skill and can be the ultimate diffuser. Sometimes disgruntled people just need to be heard. Be sure to use an example where the customer continued to be a customer.

Bonus Section

Ok, at this point, I'm going to ask you to put yourself in the recruiters' shoes. One way to do this is to "recruit" a friend or family member. Take a moment to write down how you would answer the flight attendant recruiter questions. In other words, explain to your 'partner in practice' exactly how YOU would answer these questions and have them roll play the interview with you, as YOU! Then record a mock video and watch it back so you're able to critique yourself.

They don't have to get the entire look going, but if they do, even better! Now I want YOU to play flight attendant recruiter. You will be surprised at how well this will work. You will catch so many things that you wouldn't have thought of. You might notice their posture, maybe they didn't smile or maybe they did and you see how positive that comes across. Before I was a flight attendant, I was a tour guide in Boston where I would drive a historic trolley through the city streets. Always trying to hone my craft, I would often take another drivers' tour so I could continually improve my own presentation just by paying attention to others' strengths and weaknesses. This carried over to my career in flight. When I non-revved, (non-revving is flying stand by) I would notice the great crews and I would notice the not so great crews. I was able to have a true "passengers' perspective". I can't tell you how many times I improved my own performance by spotting certain behaviors I myself, would perpetuate. It's nothing I would have noticed on my own, but seeing another flight attendant do it from a passengers' vantage point....it became glaringly obvious. I hope you can see the benefit of this activity; it's something you can have fun with and can benefit you immensely.

Here are a few example questions you can use for this activity (if you already have your questions feel free to use those as well):

• Why do you want to be a flight attendant?

• Describe a time that you handled an irate customer.

• Describe a time that you had a disagreement with a colleague.

The answers should be no longer than 2-3 minutes. They want to hear you speak clearly and concisely. They want to feel that you understand what they are asking. It is a good idea to repeat a fragment of the question back to them. For example:

Q: "Why would you like to work for xyz airline?"

A: "I would like to work for xyz airline because…"

Starting your answer with "Oh, because I've admired xyz airline my entire life. etc…" is fine and will do, but if you're as serious and committed as I think you are, you don't want to be just "fine". There is a professional courtesy in the subtle difference between the two answers. When you begin by repeating the question, you are acknowledging the fact that you are paying attention and consider the question and the questioner to be important. If it's a customer service question, don't limit your answer to just how you WOULD handle a hypothetical situation; answer with a real example of how you ACTUALLY handled a specific situation. Using the STAR method, give the S (situation) the T (task you had to complete) the A (action you took) and R (the result of the issue).

Flight Attendant Interview Checklist

2 forms of ID

A few working pens

At least 3 copies of your resume

Clear nail polish and extra pair of hose for the ladies

Watch

Passport

Breath refresher (do not chew gum at the interview)

Lipstick (ladies)

Anything else you are instructed to bring

Your warm, friendly smile! :)

Common Mistakes Aspiring Flight AttendantsMake at the Interview and How to Avoid Them!

Mistake #1 Arriving Late. This may seem obvious and you may think it's not worth mentioning, but you'd be surprised at how many people show up exactly when the interview is starting or even 5 minutes before. When you have an interview you need to be there at least 5 minuted before it starts. I recommend 15 minutes ahead of time. Think of it this way, if you show up for a 3pm departure at 3pm, the door will be closed. You are not on time, unless you are early.

Mistake #2 Leaving your electronics on. Another easy mistake to make, but it is an important detail. Turn off your phone before entering the building. You do not want to be the one with the ringing phone as the the recruiters start the session.

Mistake #3 Only Silencing Your Phone. Don't just silence your phone, turn it off. It will be too tempting to check Instagram or update Facebook. You are being watched from the time you arrive until you leave. The recruiters want to see that you are aware of your surroundings, interested in what's going on around you and engaged in the environment you're in. Be social, talk to the other potential flight attendants. The recruiters want to know you are comfortable in new social situations.

Mistake #4 Not Being Dressed for an Interview. Another common mistake. This is an easy one to get right, yet so many get this one wrong. Recruiters are left to ask themselves, does this person, with no hose, wearing open toed sandals think they're special or have they not done their research? Neither answer leaves a lot of confidence that this person is the right choice for the job.

Mistake #5 Not Engaging with Others. Flight Attendant Recruiters are assessing you from the moment they see you. You don't need to take over the room when you walk in, but smile, say hello to everyone you make eye contact with. Engage in light conversation, but avoid gossiping about the airline or the interview process.

Mistake #6 Lack of Confidence. Fake it 'til ya make it! Being confident and self assured is a huge part of being a flight attendant. You work with new people all the time, you are the frontline employee of the airline and you work unsupervised. You also wear many "hats" as a flight attendant and are often called on to make decisions that aren't in a manual. Show confidence by making eye contact, listening when spoken to and being aware of your body language. No slouching or nervous ticks!

Mistake #7 Using one word answers. When answering the interview questions you need to elaborate. If asked if you've ever dealt with an irate customer, don't just say yes. This is the time to give an example and how you were able to successfully diffuse the situation.

Mistake #8 Asking How Long Reserve is. This is the recruiters time to find out if you have what it takes to be a flight attendant. Save questions about reserve, relocating and salary for after you are offered an invite to training. If the recruiter brings up any of these things be careful how you respond. If you would like the chance to think about whether you want this job or not, watch your reaction. The only correct response at this point is, you are willing to live anywhere, be on reserve forever and Ramen Noodles is your favorite food;)

Q&A with a Flight Attendant Recruiter

Q. **Please explain how a typical day of flight attendant interviews is run.**

A. The process is constantly changing based on the number of applicants arriving that day AND the number of recruiters staffed for the day. The basics remain the same: You will be welcomed into a holding room and asked for a copy of your resume and any letters of recommendation and referrals. The group will see a short presentation about the airline and then be able to ask questions regarding the position and the expectations of being on reserve. The face to face interview will take place in another room and applicants are called randomly for that process.

Q. **Do first impressions really make a difference?**

A. YES! It's a popular quote for a reason. You DO only have one chance to make a good impression. Remember that the recruiters may be all around the building you are interviewing in. You have no idea who you'll be speaking with, so assume that each person you come in contact with might be a decision maker. There will always be that one candidate who might not get an offer because of something that was observed outside of the actual interview process. ex) talking loudly on a cell phone, cursing where someone might hear you, inappropriate conversations not suitable for a business setting, not seeming to be interested in what others are saying, setting up a complete "beauty salon" in a public restroom, arriving in overly casual attire, changing in a public restroom, etc.

Q. **When a flight attendant candidate enters the room what do you typically notice first?**

A. Approachability — the natural warmth and engaging smile PLUS the overall polish of the entire look. We are hiring people that greet our customers and care for them. Do they look like and act like they care? We wear uniforms. Do they look natural and comfortable in business attire? Are the tags cut off the clothing or are they wearing it for the occasion and returning it? Is the vent tack sewn on the back of the jacket cut open? Have they thought through the whole look? Do the clothes fit? If they don't, we must question whether they will represent the uniform well.

Q. How should a recruit be dressed?

A. That's a tough one as we hire folks dressed in many different fashions. We understand that a 21 year old may have a completely different professional style that a 50 year old person. Basic rule of thumb: "Conservative and professional". Men: Suit or Blazer with slacks/dress shirt/tie/polished shoes. Women: Suit, Jacket/skirt combo, Dress with sleeves and a jacket, closed toe shoes with a short heel, conservative/simple jewelry.

We want to feel confident that you will represent the uniform well and represent the brand with a polished and professional look, overall. AVOID: casual attire, sundresses, anything revealing, skirts that are above the knee, long nails, flashy or glittery nail polish, excessive jewelry, excessive cologne, tight clothing, cleavage revealing blouses, very high heels, non-business style purses overflowing with personal effects, casual backpacks (men in a suit with a backpack look like children going off to school!), trendy accessories, multiple earrings.

Q. What types of interviews does your airline have? Please explain each.

A. The video interview comes first. Use the practice time available to see how you look into the camera on your computer or phone. Dress for the interview. Avoid distracting backgrounds or interruptions. We are looking for people at this point to be well spoken, articulate, approachable, genuine, and poised. There will be a specific time allowed for each answer; do not feel you have to use up every second. If you do, you're probably babbling and saying way more than is necessary.

If you pass the video interview, there is a face to face interview that may or may not conclude with a second face to face interview - depending on the day.

Q. If you do have two interviewers interviewing a candidate, what is the purpose of having two?

A. Having 2 interviewers allows two people to take notes at the same time and compare their findings. We've done it both ways here and we found that after a recruiter was trained, the decisions were virtually the same. Currently, we still do both single and double, depending on the staffing and the numbers who interview that day.

Q. What kind of work and/or life experience are you looking for in a candidate?

A. At least 2 years in customer service.

Q. Should a potential candidate bring his or her resume with them to the interview? If so, what are you looking for on the resume? How long should it be?

A. YES! Bring several copies. This way the recruiter can review one and you'll have extra in case they gets creased or you spill something on one. Don't arrive and ask the recruiter to print one for you. Yes, you sent one in with your application but we will not print it out for you. The directions clearly state you must bring it with you. You would not believe the stories we get about why candidates don't have them.

If possible, make the resume one page. There is no reason to list all the duties of every job you had. Simple and clear is best. List the dates at each job with month and year. If there are large gaps, be prepared to explain. If there are multiple jobs in a short amount of time, be prepared to be asked why you left. Be honest.

As a recruiter, I spend very little time on the resume because it is not nearly important as what is sitting in front of me. However, if it is thrown together, messy, soiled, or full of misspellings, I'm inclined to think the applicant doesn't really care about getting the job.

Q. Do things like posture and eye contact matter during the interview?

A. Yes, I'm constantly thinking how would this person appear to our customers?

Q. Does it help or hinder to have a recommendation letter from a current flight attendant?

A. I think it helps, rarely hinders, but does not become a huge part of the process. The interview is still the deciding factor with the referral being an added part in the plus column.

Q. If a FA candidate is currently employed with another airline as a flight attendant, what are some good reasons to be seeking employment at your airline? What kind of reasons would disqualify them from being hired and what kind of reasons would be acceptable?

A. I've heard every reason possible. Good? Moving from express to mainline so they can fly more destinations and work with more people. They've always admired our airline. They are limited at their carrier by its smaller size.

Q. Describe your ideal candidate.

A. Polished and articulate professional who is modern, fresh, and excited about changes that are inevitable in an airline job. They truly WANT the job. One who understands, and is ok with the pay structure and that the starting pay is extremely low. They have thought through the possibility that it might be years on reserve and years before they can transfer to the city of their choice. They must be customer focused and natural problem solvers — not just "nice".

Q. Do you use the STAR method?

A. We do use the STAR (situation, task, action, result) method. I can smell a canned answer from a mile away and those who practice instead of allowing themselves to be natural on that day often bomb their interview. There are websites that give the questions and I can't tell you how many applicants come in with the answers basically memorized from those websites. They might be good applicants but since I don't have any real data to go on, they fail the interview. There is nothing wrong with thinking through situations you have been involved in, but when the answer is the same example I got from the last two applicants, something is wrong. Also, I never trust someone who says they've never had a difficult situation at work.

Remember this is just a jumping off point! If you are serious about investing in yourself and fulfilling your dream of becoming a flight attendant, check out our services at:

www.theflightattendantcourse.com
Sara@theflightattendantcourse.com

Made in United States
North Haven, CT
16 June 2023

37837490R00020